The Strange Animal Farm

LaShawna Fant

Limits of Liability and Disclaimer of Warranty

The author and publisher shall not be liable for your misuse of this material. This book is strictly for informational purposes. The purpose of this book is to educate and entertain. The author and publisher do not guarantee anyone following these techniques, suggestions, tips, ideas, or strategies will become successful. The author and publisher shall have neither liability nor responsibility to anyone with respect to any loss or damage caused, or alleged to be caused, directly or indirectly by the information contained in this book. Views expressed in this publication do not necessarily reflect the views of the publisher.

Printed in the United States of America

Keen Vision Publishing, LLC

www.keen-vision.com

ISBN: 978-1-948270-34-2

For my inspirations and loves forever: Darius, Nikki, and Vicki Fant. And for my hometown, Houston, Mississippi & the community of Mantee, Mississippi.

There is a shark
Whose name is Mark.
He likes to bark
At the park
When it is dark.

There is a hen
Who likes to count to ten
And write with her pen
While sitting in her den.

There is a kangaroo
Who likes to moo
And eat stew.
His favorite color is blue
And he enjoys having gum that he can chew
While using sticky glue.

There are three peacocks
Who like playing with big blocks
Sticking keys in locks
And wearing purple socks.
The peacocks travel in huge flocks
And make clocks
While sitting on small rocks.

There is a mouse
Who lives in a tall house
And likes wearing a yellow blouse.

There is a yak
Who is black
And likes to quack.
He hangs his clothes on a rack
And every day he packs a snack
In which he puts in a sack.

There are two crocodiles
Who fold towels and place them in piles.
They greet people with smiles
When they are outside walking long miles.

There is a snail
Who reads braille
Drinks juice from a pale
And rings her cowbell.

There is a toad
Who always carries a heavy load
While walking down the railroad.

There are goats
Who wear coats
And write notes
While traveling in their boats.

There is a rat
Who sleeps on a striped mat
Wears a hat
And his friend is the cat.
Every day they chat
With the gnat
Make pancakes that are flat
And play baseball with a bat.

There is a crow
Who wears a red bow
In her huge afro.
She likes to throw
Balls made of snow
And to row
While playing with Play-Doh.

There is a bear
That has wild hair
And sits in his wooden chair
While eating a green pear.

There is a snake
Who likes to bake
And eat strawberry cake.
The snake uses his rake
To clean up leaves around the lake
While drinking a milkshake.

There is a hog
Whose best friend is the dog.
They like to jog
Rest afterwards on a log
And chat with the frog.

There is a pig
Who is pretty big!
She likes to chew on a fig
And wear her pink and lime green wig
While playing drums with a twig.

There are three elephants
Who are good friends with the ants.
The elephants wear orange pants
Scream funny chants
And water their plants.

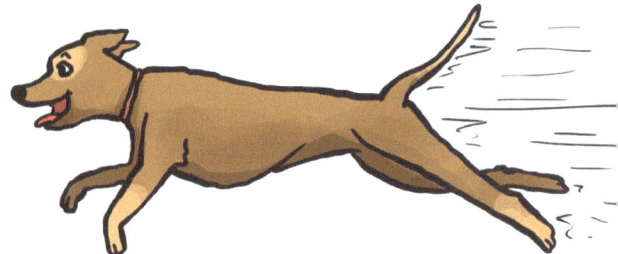

There is a mole
Who eats his food out of a bowl.
He likes to kick his football through a goal
And fish at the pond using a pole.

There is a duck
Who always has one buck.
He drives a purple truck
And believes in good luck.

There is a red fish
Who likes to make a wish
And eats out of a round dish.

There is a bumblebee
Who drinks sweet tea
While eating a black-eyed pea.
He likes to count to three
And uses a key
To open the door to his house that is in a tree.

There is a fly
Who wears a blue bowtie
While flying in the sky
As a private spy.
He likes to eat apple pie
Food that he can fry
And bread made of rye.

There is a cow
Who loves to chow
And always takes a bow
When using his plow.

There is a deer
Who drinks root beer
And likes to do a cheer
While wearing football gear.

There is a sheep
Who likes to sweep
And takes a big leap
When getting out of his green jeep.

There is a mule
Who is always breaking a rule.
She wears a scarf made of wool
And a big green jewel.

There is an ape
Who plays with tape
Wears a red cape
And is always eating
on one green grape.

There is a skunk
Who sleeps in a trunk
Collects a lot of junk
And likes to dunk.

There is a ladybug
Who lives under a rug
Drinks milk out of a jug
Chugs coffee down out of her mug
And enjoys receiving a big hug.

There is a bunny
Who likes eating honey
Counting her money
Being outside when it is sunny
And telling a lot of jokes that are funny.

There is a dolphin
Who has a long chin
Likes to grin
And when playing sports, he likes to win.

There are three nice mice
Who eat rice
Cheese pizza by the slice
And always drink lemonade with a lot of ice.

There is a ram
Whose best friend is the lamb.
The ram loves to eat ham
On which he spreads peach jam.

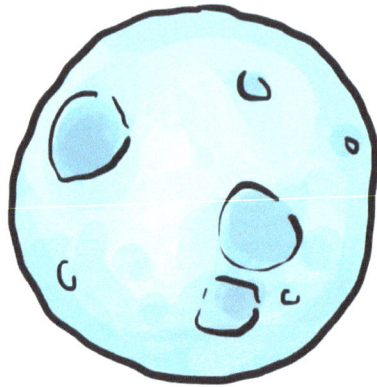

There is a raccoon
Who is friends with the baboon.
The raccoon likes watching a funny cartoon
Playing outside around noon
Looking at a full moon
And eating food with a big spoon.

About the Author

Houston, Mississippi born Dr. LaShawna Fant is devoted to giving her readers larger than life stories sprinkled with her southern charm. Dr. Fant is an educator, counselor, and serves in many roles within the community of individuals who are living with blindness. The Strange Animal Farm is the first book published by Dr. Fant. It colorfully invites children to visit the unique farm to meet the human-like animals.

Stay Connected

Thank you for reading The Strange Animal Farm. LaShawna Fant looks forward to connecting with you and keeping you updated on her next releases. Below are a few ways you can connect with the author.

Facebook Author Page- LaShawna Fant
Email lashawnafant@yahoo.com
Website www.lfantbooks.com

www.ingramcontent.com/pod-product-compliance
Lightning Source LLC
LaVergne TN
LVHW072132070426
835513LV00002B/74

9 781948 270342